THE

AWAKENED WINNERS

We Already Won

Loida Dominguez

Dedication

Nicholis, did you know that I found love for me through loving you?

Before you were thought of I smoked cigarettes, I drank alcohol almost every day and hung out with people that did drugs and or sold them.

After finding out you were coming into the world all of that changed. I stopped smoking, something I tried to do so many times and did it in a second for you. I stopped drinking and my surroundings changed because of those decisions.

I wanted to know God more than ever before. I wanted to ensure that I'd be my best self so that I could be that for you. I accomplished so much for us. Because my life was no longer only about me and when it was, I didn't treat myself like I mattered.

With you by my side I remembered my love for me. I remembered that my life matters and that I could love myself in ways I hadn't before. In loving your heartbeat, I began to listen to and love my own.

Nicholis, you were brought to me for a reason. One huge reason is to help me remember LOVE, and through that I found my purpose and for that I am so absolutely grateful. Because of your presence I chose to change and in turn I saved my life.

Your presence has had a tremendous impact on my life. You are a gift to me and the world. The world is a better place because you are in it.

My prayer is that the world knows how magnificent you are, as they remember how magnificent they are. Because anyone that doesn't see your magnificence, doesn't see their own.

I Love You Forevaaaa......

Preface

Hello, my name is Loida Dominguez, and I am here to share a wonderful journey with you—a journey full of exploration and awakening to deep, abundant, and whole love. You know the type of love that you are in each moment. You were born with inherent worth, and I will guide you to remember just that and more. I know that you are ready to take a deep dive, and I'm excited for us and the journey we are about to take together. I hope you are excited too!

It took me a while to get clear on how to write the information that follows because I pondered on what would be the best way to relay the message, and then I realized that those who get it will, and those who don't won't, and that is okay. My service is to help people see their wholeness as a force of one body. If you are not aware of that yet, then my hope is that after you read this, you will be, and that, if you are aware, this will encourage and strengthen your belief.

My desire is to help more people awaken to both darkness and light within, so that we stop projecting our worst or best onto the outside world. Because when we project our worst or best, we create a mess out there. By doing our own individual work inside, we create space for true love to arise.

My message is about transforming the way that you see and

feel. There is nothing pretty about living small. Your presence is invaluable and being alive says you are worthy of love. Learning to love yourself unconditionally will help you celebrate all that you are in each moment, which is what I believe is intended for all of us. Coming home to oneself is an amazing journey, one that I share wholeheartedly as an offering so that I, too, may help others awaken just as I was helped by many.

Let us stop reaching for a truth that already exists inside of us. Let us stop begging for answers when we are both the question and the answer. Let us feel the privilege of existence as we express the ultimate gratitude for each moment, and let us let go, allow and fully trust that we are held and loved, just as we are.

Contents

Dedication i

Preface iii

Chapter 1: **Is This Love** 1

Chapter 2: **Internal Observation** 21

Chapter 3: **Hero-In** 35

Chapter 4: **Masculine and Feminine Forces** 57

Chapter 5: **Behind the Mirror** 65

Chapter 6: **Awaken** 85

Chapter 7: **We Already Won** 97

Acknowledgments 107

About the Author 111

Chapter 1

Is This Love

When most of what you see around you is pain, you begin to question, "What is love?" Or at least I know that's what I did. When I was a child, I experienced many painful things that left me questioning, "Is this love?" In fact, I recall waking up one morning when I was about six years old, looking at my mother and saying, "Mom I don't believe in God." I immediately started to cry. I know that for some this wouldn't be a big deal, but it was and is for me. I wonder, how much pain I was experiencing to stop believing in a higher power at the age of six?

It is said that suffering is of the mind, but what if most people aren't aware of that? And what if, because of this lack of awareness, we create more pain in ourselves and in the world around us?

As a child, I was surrounded by many of what I call "lost children." Children in adult bodies, unaware that the solutions they were seeking were inside of themselves.

I grew up watching adults consuming alcohol like water. I

grew up watching adults desperately taking medication to cope. I grew up watching adults using drugs and alcohol to numb their pain.

I had no adult role model or anyone that had the awareness to guide me to the vast and beautiful world that resides within me. I recall going to family parties when I was a child, watching my family get drunk and then physically fight with each other. Could you imagine my younger cousins, siblings and I, witnessing this at every family party we went to? Where were the adults? The adults were busy creating the pain they were trying to escape.

There was a moment at one of the parties I can never forget because what I saw was unbearable. I was brought once again to a family party to watch yet another fight, but this one was different because one of my sisters was in it. I heard screams, "Let her go!" Then the screams got louder: "Let her go!" "Let her go!" They were screaming so my aunt would release my sister's finger from her clenched teeth. An ambulance was called for my sister, whose finger was bitten until it broke.

Is this love? Can somebody tell me, is this love? I'm a child, lost alone and afraid. The adults around me are lost children too. They are in adult bodies, functioning from their wounds. So where is the adult that can model healthy relationships for me? The one that can show and guide me to know what love is. Somebody? Anybody? Can somebody tell me, is this love?

I AM LOVE, YOU ARE
LOVE, WE ARE LOVE AND
WE ARE LOVED

Awakening To Love

I have realized that most of us are taught how not to love. Therefore the chaos in our lives is created by an illusionary love. This is where the term lost child comes in because we get lost trying to find our way back to the magical truth of what love really is.

There are many misconceptions created in our world. Some of those misconceptions are created by our interpretations. Such as the stories, scriptures, and myths that tell us the *truth*. The reason I highlight truth is because there are so many; yet the truth is what we accept and believe to be true. For example, I can say a paper is black, and I can be certain of that, and that becomes my truth. You can say it's white and be certain of that, and that becomes your truth; and so it is. My purpose then isn't to try to change what you believe, but to be present with your dream as you see it. It is then that there is room for both of us to evolve from simply being present with someone else's point of view. What a powerful notion this truly is because it means we don't have to do or say anything; therefore, there is no attachment to what we call truth. It is just that—our truth.

You might say "But the paper is black," or "The paper is white." Of course, that may be true in your eyes but what do we get from being right? For many, it is believed that being right is fulfilling, and it is, but only to the ego. If the ego is what we fill, then we will hunger for more of being right so that we feel righteous, whole and complete, and in the midst of that, we miss the entire dream. We forget that we are already whole and complete, and we miss the moment that is being offered right now.

Right now is really all we have, and everything else is an illusion. A past dream that is gone and cannot be touched, or a future dream that is far ahead and cannot be touched either. We can imagine a change in the past, but what will that serve if the past cannot be changed? We can also focus all of our attention on a future goal that doesn't guarantee anything, or we can be here, meeting life right where it is.

I'm not suggesting you don't create goals and go for them, but I am suggesting that you notice if and when you are being run by them. Where is your attention? When your attention is in the past or future, will you be with the tension of the desire to go back or forth and stay in the center where choice and your true power live.

Be in alignment with right here, right now and be free!

YOU ARE NOW

The Journey

We arrive from a long ride in and through the fallopian tubes as sperm to meet the egg. From there, we transform to begin to experience our humanity. Wherever evolution takes us, we transform over and over again. Every second, we die as we shed and open to the new. Whether it be a new second, a new way of being, or a new state of consciousness, as we become more aware of ourselves, we die only to live again. With every breath that we breathe, we make room for the next, and so it is.

We come into the world small, new, and unsure of anything other than the impact that the experience of being born has on us. The lights, the cold, the sound of our cry; we are born anew, experiencing everything for the first time in this form, our body, the temple that is the home to our soul. What a precious one, the home to our divinity, and the reminder that we are Spirit in a body. We expand to contract, and we contract only to expand, and so it is.

We begin our journey alive, conscious, awake, with a stream of energy in us, through us, and around us. Then we begin to experience life, on the terms that are handed to us by our caretakers, family, friends, and the society around us. We grow up and develop the capacity to choose who and how we want to be according to our experiences.

When we are born, we are immediately assigned a gender, and most of us are taught to dress, look, and feel a certain way according to our family or societal norms. For many girls, this means you wear mostly pink dresses, you are a pretty girl, you always act like a lady and are guided toward ballet and fairy tales. For many boys, this means you wear mostly blue, you are cute, you are tough, and you are guided toward sports.

This is not to say that these activities should be stopped because, truth be told, I think they're amazing. I bring them up to bring awareness of how some things are forced on some of us. We are guided toward an identity chosen by our caretakers and society. Then we deem our truth to be the reality created for us, and this is just the beginning of the conditioned mind.

Who Am I

As a child, I expressed my truth by ways of celebrating myself and at times I was told that it's wrong. I learned to hide myself, and in the midst of it all, I lost my true identity. You see, there comes a time when some of the experiences many of us have become way too difficult to bear. It becomes too difficult to want to be seen, felt, heard, and loved as we realize that not many things give to those experiences. We learn to work so hard to get the love we were born with, and we lose the reality of love in the form that we are in every moment.

The Awakened Winners

Many of us begin to create barriers of protection when we are way too young to understand what it is that we are doing. We go through painful experiences, and we learn to hide behind masks because we become too afraid to show our true selves. For some, there was no choice but to do this because the personas created were for survival.

This is something that happens for all of us in some way. Becoming aware of this has helped me see myself, my parents, siblings, extended family and humanity with love and compassion. I understand that we all do the best that we can until we know a better way. Then we do better because we know better.

Next, I will give some examples of situations that become the reasons for the creation of our masks. Some you will be able to relate to, and some you won't. Either way, I ask that you keep your heart open as you read. I share these to bring awareness because if we can see, we can choose how we want to be in the world.

I also want to share that I realize that it is easier to see my experiences and not as easy to see what I have offered as an experience. I share this to bring awareness to both victims and victimizers. These dualities live within us. Without awareness we project our internal battle and create wars. Therefore, true transformation is seen from the inside out.

Lastly, I have chosen genders for what I share but know that either experience has and can happen to both girls and boys.

Big Girls Don't Cry

A little girl is playing in the park with her friends. She's running around, having a great time, when suddenly she trips and falls, scraping her knee. She cries as she runs to her dad, who's sitting at a bench nearby.

"Daddy," she says, with tears running down her cheek, "I fell, and it hurts."

The father looks at the little girl with concern in his eyes and says, "Let me see." He then grabs a napkin, wipes the blood off of her knee, and says, "Oh, it's not too bad, go on, wipe your tears. Big girls don't cry."

The girl proceeds to wipe her tears, while limping back to the playground. Her friends see her and run toward her, asking, "Are you okay?"

The young girl wipes her face and says, "Yes, I'm okay. Big girls don't cry." The young girl grows up refusing to display sadness or pain because she is attached to the belief that tears are a sign of weakness.

I'm not enough

A little boy comes home from school with homework. He sits with his mom in the kitchen, where there is space for her to help him. They begin to work on his math homework. The boy is doing well until he stumbles upon a problem that he has a difficult time solving.

The mother tries to help him solve the problem with no success. She gets frustrated and begins to shout, "Really? You don't know this? What's wrong with you? This is easy."

The boy puts his head down and begins to weep, making it harder for him to see the problem on the sheet.

The mother then stomps out of the room, shouting, "I'm done, I don't want to deal with this anymore," leaving her child alone, feeling unloved, when he is simply struggling to find the answer. A child left feeling helpless and hopeless, he grows up feeling ashamed and unworthy of love.

Saying bye to being quiet and shy

A young teen girl is sitting at her desk at school, when two of her classmates begin to speak loudly next to her, saying things such as, "She's ugly. Don't you just want to punch her?"

The girl sits there, afraid, hoping they would go away. Then one of the bullies knocks her hat off of her head and proceeds to try to take her glasses off. Shortly after, the girl sums up some courage and looks at the bullies angrily. They look back at her, laugh, and one of them jabs, "You're scared, huh?"

The other bully responds, "Yeah, she is scared."

The bullies then push the girl's desk, leaving the girl feeling sad and scared. The bullies keep calling her names and pushing her desk until the young teen girl gets up from her chair frustrated and yells, "ENOUGH ALREADY!" She then goes home, changes her clothes, and puts on her tough girl personality, never to be that quiet, shy little girl again. She realized she has to toughen up if she wants to survive in school, and that is exactly what she does.

Adult child

A father stumbles in at 3 a.m. after he had been out drinking all night. His wife was awake in bed, feeling disappointed at the pattern her husband had been on for way too long. She gets up from her bed to approach him about his actions. She finds him on the kitchen floor and says, "You know what? I have had it. I'm done, I don't want to do this anymore."

The husband manages to get himself back on his feet and responds with, "What are you talking about? You are overreacting."

They begin to scream back and forth, the wife yells at him to leave, and the husband responds, "No, this is my home."

Their two children wake up because of the screams. The youngest child, a seven-year-old girl, says to her twelve-year-old brother, "I'm scared," and she begins to cry.

The brother comforts the little girl and says, "Don't be scared. Stay here. I'll be right back." He then goes to the kitchen, where both parents are yelling at one another, and screams, "Will you both stop it? Grow up already!" The parents both stop and look at the child with disbelief. They know that their child is picking up a role that doesn't belong to him; he was becoming an adult before his time.

These are just a few experiences that we have that give rise to the makings of our personality masks. We all go through experiences that bring us to create masks. Then we wonder why we are not seen for who we are, when truth be told, most of us don't know ourselves. We create mask after mask, and then we go out into society with our preferred mask on and we mostly greet other people's masks. This is how most of humanity functions—politics are run this way, and our children learn from us how to be in the world. That is why I took the initiative to go through my healing process so that I can help others awaken too, for I know that the more people awaken, the more we help the beautiful world we live in. In doing so, we create a better environment and future for our children.

I SEE THE LIGHT IN
YOUR EYES

Perception of Perfection

What is perfection? To many, it is said that there is no such thing as perfect, but what if there is? And what if most of us have a distorted point of view of perfection? I believe we are perfect, in each moment our best self, but if we imagine perfection to be anything other than what we are, we go chasing for what we deem perfection to be.

I recall being picked on as a child. I was told, among many things, that my smile wasn't perfect, so I closed myself in, I stopped smiling or I covered my mouth when I laughed. I created many masks growing up because I took other people's perception of perfection as my own. I gave my power away, and in doing so, I lost myself. Of course, as a child, I was not aware of the power of perception, but now I see it clearly. Although many of the experiences I had as a child were painful for me, I can see now how they all served me because, through the pain, I learned to love deeply, and I'm grateful for the way that I love.

PERFECTION IS WHAT WE ARE!

Life after Birth

When I found out I was pregnant, I honestly was devastated. I was in an unhealthy relationship and wanted out. I cried when I saw a positive pregnancy test. I thought "what do I do? Do I keep the baby?" So many questions ran through my mind, but I took my time to decide.

I remember going to the doctor for my first ultrasound. As soon as I saw the image of what looked like a bean on the screen, I cried. I knew at that moment that I was in love with the life that was growing within me. There was no more struggle after that. I knew that I was keeping my baby.

I carried my baby for nine months, not knowing his gender by choice; I wanted it to be a surprise. The experience of carrying a baby without knowing any details about it, yet loving it so much, was what I know now to be unconditional love. I had never loved that strongly, and to not see or know anything about my child but to know with all certainty that I was in love, was by far one of the most amazing experiences of my life.

The day my baby was about to arrive, I was in a lot of pain, and I was anxious to hold him or her in my arms. Finally, my baby was here, and when it was born, the doctor stated, "It's a boy, and he was born with Down Syndrome."

At that moment, I looked at my baby boy as the doctor held him and I reached out my hands to hold my beautiful son, as if saying with no words, "Giveth here that precious child of mine." I remember thinking he had the most perfectly round-shaped head, and I couldn't stop looking at his fingers and toes. I was completely in love, and it was such a blessing to finally hold him in my arms.

These moments shifted quickly, as the experience I had after his diagnosis became confusing for me. Not because of his diagnosis, but more so because of how some people received the news. I realized that this was another opportunity for me to experience the perception of perfection. Especially because for me my son was perfect.

I recall one person asking me, "Do you think he was born with Down syndrome because of you or his dad?" as if asking who is to blame for this perceived imperfection, or "Aww, poor baby, I will pray for him." As if my son was someone to feel sorry for. I even had one person ask me, "Why do you think this happened to you? You are such a good person!" Yes, someone said that to me, as if someone must be a bad person to have a child with Down Syndrome. This all goes to show how little most of us know about true love. I feel sad as I write, and this is it; the perception of perfection is the perception that someone should be different according to our point of view.

We all have our own perception of perfection, and it comes from how we perceive ourselves. Without this awareness many of us judge people for the color of their skin, the religion they practice, their sexual orientation, disabilities and more. This occurs when we imagine we aren't whole, complete, love and loved. The judgments made aren't about the people that are judged, they are about the ones judging. How are we supposed to see perfection in another if we can't see it in ourselves?

I wrote the following quote a few years ago, and I feel it is fitting to share it with you here: "We can spend a lifetime trying to perfect a heart that is already perfect, or we can see the perfection in the heart and love it for a lifetime." Know, see, and love yourself in every moment as the perfection that you are. You are love and loved in this moment and you are this moment. When we live from this awareness and knowing, all we can see, feel, and experience is love because every moment is new and perfect, as are you.

I SEE YOU THE WAY THAT I SEE MYSELF

Chapter 2

Internal Observation

Before I continue to the next phase of my book, I want to share an analogy that's been helpful for me and my clients. It has served us to be present in our lives. I'll share my analogy with you shortly. First, I want to share that prior to journeying inward I found myself with a lot of anxiety and felt depressed often. So, I put myself through an internal observation process to find out what life is truly about. I analyzed my thoughts and mental patterns to see, feel, and experience my true power.

When I fully understood that I am not my thoughts, feelings, emotions, or experiences, I felt the freedom that comes with knowing that this moment is really all there is. I realized my heart is the steering wheel of my life, my body the vehicle and I am the driver.

I now understand that we are always directing our lives but many of us are doing so without awareness. We are mostly creating more of what we don't want because we don't even know that we are running the show.

When we are not aware, we are lost, not knowing who we are. We are trapped, believing that life is happening to us, versus the truth that life is happening for us. We are co-creating with life, and we are seeded here as life to experience ourselves as love in every moment. The unfortunate thing is that without awareness we live most of our lives rejecting what is so generously being offered to us. The wonderful thing is that by becoming aware, we will shift ourselves and the energy of our beloved planet.

The Web

Imagine yourself as a spider, creating a web. You are slowly spinning your web and as you complete it, you suddenly feel stuck. You can't move, so you begin to try to figure out how to get out of the web. As a spider you can move on the web freely but because you think you're the web, you feel stuck.

This is what many of us do, except we do it with our thoughts. We get thoughts, we claim them and without awareness we believe we are them. As we become aware of this pattern, we detach from an imagined reality, and we step into the power of choice. With awareness, we are free to create what we desire and there is so much power in that.

The web analogy is to help you see that you are the creator of your story. When you are not aware of this, you attach to a story that doesn't serve you to live the life that you desire.

I will be using the web analogy often to give you visuals of what you may be doing with your thoughts. The definition of The Web, as I will be using it throughout my book is; Any thought we attach our identity to. Whether it be the thought that we are losers because we lost something externally, or winners because we won something externally. Both identifying factors keep us reaching for something to complete our sense of self. Without awareness we give our power to those identities. Then we lean away from our wholeness because we are attached to the imagination that wholeness is something other than what we are.

What I have written will offer you many opportunities to reflect on things you may be attaching yourself to. I have written short stories to help you see yourself in ways you may not have yet. I recommend that you take your time as you read and allow things to land without rushing. I also want to take this moment to thank you for allowing me the privilege of impacting you and possibly opening your heart wider than ever before.

Railing Against

Have you ever railed against the weather? Such as, "Snow, again? Ugh."

Most people will answer, "Yes, I have railed against the weather, and many other things too."

I want to be clear that the problem isn't in having a preference. The problem is in attaching to the imagination that things are bad because they are not what we prefer.

When we attach our identity to the web we see life through the lens of our perception of perfection. In doing so we forget that we are the perfection that's creating the web. We forget that we are the ones entertaining the thoughts that come through us. Therefore, we live our lives seeing imperfections everywhere.

In fact, I will share a story that is beyond perfect for this analogy: I was at my old job, working at an after-school program. At some point one of the children looked outside and saw a tree had broken branches after enduring some winter storms.

After looking at the tree for a while, the young girl said out loud, "Aww, that tree used to be so perfect."

I was curious about her statement and thought, "What if the tree is perfect as it is now? And what if it is our perception of perfection that has us lose sight of that?"

Shortly after that, I shared what came up for me with the young girl, and she asked, "What do you mean?"

I then told her that I believe perfection to be a point of view.

You see, I believe most human beings do the same thing the young girl did with the tree. We judge things, people, and situations as imperfect through a lens that isn't truly who or what we are. We see life through our perception of perfection, and we make a mess out of the perfection that is.

I reflected a lot on the tree that the little girl pointed out as imperfect. Especially because I know that many people project imperfection onto someone that doesn't have limbs. The same goes for people with scars, disabilities, people that are too tall, too small, too wide, too thin, too much, not enough, the list goes on.

To see with the eyes of love is to see perfection in everything and everyone. When we become aware that railing against people, things or situations only keeps us stuck. We regain our power because we come back home to the one, we are in control of. It is then that we detach from the illusion that people, things, or situations are separate from us. Therefore, we begin to see perfection in ourselves and in doing so, we begin to see perfection in others as well.

Meaning-Making Fiesta

One of the many things I was doing without awareness was attaching a meaning to everything. I was taught that everything has a meaning or reason behind it, so every time something happened, I would look for the reason. This became my addiction. "I must know the meaning, because everything happens for a reason." This was like having a fiesta for my mind every day, except the "fiesta" wasn't always fun for me.

I would experience highs when I knew and lows when I didn't know. I realized that I associated knowing with winning and not knowing with losing, so I fought long and hard to know.

I now understand that winning isn't anything other than an attachment to the imagination of what it means to win. Therefore I no longer have fiestas that keep me trapped in a web of lies. I have fiestas that are based on the truth. I am a winner and so are you.

Who's Driving?

As I observed the many things I'd attach to, there was one that really stuck out for me. It was based on how I entertain my thoughts and attach to them as truth. I had this realization as I drove my car. I was driving and I noticed what I would do that would induce much anxiety for me. I will explain it to you by having you imagine you are driving a car. As you drive, you have both hands on the steering wheel. You are driving along, and you suddenly get a thought you prefer not to have, so you pick up the thought by removing one hand from the steering wheel. Now you are driving with one hand on the steering wheel, while the other hand is holding a thought.

Then, as you reject that fear-based thought, your body goes into protection mode because your mind doesn't know the difference between true danger and a thought of something dangerous. Because you are not aware of this, your reaction to your body symptoms would be to ask, "What's wrong with me?" In that moment, when you ask that question, you pick up a feeling.

Now both of your hands are off the steering wheel. You look at the steering wheel and ask, "Who's driving?" The answer to that question is, "the web" which, in this case, is your car, and it's driving with no one directing it because you are holding two delusions, and you are identified with those delusions as if they are you.

Drop It

From this awareness, you can begin to drop what you pick up as truth. You can witness your thoughts by observing them, which means you can notice when you pick up a thought, and you can simply choose to drop it. Guide yourself to drop what you have picked up and, while doing that, feel yourself less in your head and more in your body.

You see, many of us get identified with our thoughts and we create a reality according to them. If this is you, know that you don't have to do this anymore? You have awareness, and where there is awareness, there is choice. Remember that your thoughts only have power over you when you give your power to them. You can stop obsessive thinking by giving your full attention to what's in front of you right now.

Our obsessive thinking comes from habitually jumping on the thought train and going for a ride, which is likely a habit that has been practiced for years. The good news is that, by practicing something new, you can create a habit that better serves you to experience true freedom.

Memory

Something that induces a memory response or reaction, is known as a trigger. When we have a strong reaction to an experience now, it often comes from something we experienced in the past. Without awareness we project our past onto present times, and we react to current situations from a memory. As adults we try to resolve our childhood wounds by trying to forcefully change our present reality. The pain we experience from the memory feels so strong that we imagine there is no other way. Therefore, we get swept into believing that we are our past experiences.

What I have learned through my process is that when I become aware of my past pain, I am no longer caught in the grip of my reaction. You see, you are only caught in bondage when you let an automatic trigger response get a hold of you, as if what was triggered by your memory is happening again in the moment.

A scent, a person, or an experience can induce an automatic memory response. By becoming aware we can let go of the spiraling thoughts that may occur when triggered.

Therefore, alleviating the feelings, senses, and emotions that were induced by the attachment to the memory. This doesn't mean "let's stop feeling;" it means we notice where the reality of the feeling is coming from. If it's a memory response, it is happening in your mind. With this awareness you can shift from being engulfed in your thoughts by remembering that you are the spider and the creator of the web. Strengthen your awareness by getting curious about your thoughts and the feelings, senses, and emotions that come through as you think something.

Replay

Have you ever been somewhere, listening to music, and then suddenly a love song comes on and you not only start to sing it, but you also start to live it? As in this example: I went through a breakup, and a few weeks later, I heard the song *So Sick* by Ne-Yo. He sings, "And I'm so sick of love songs, so tired of tears / So done with wishing you were still here / Said I'm so sick of love songs, so sad and slow / Why can't I turn off the radio?" (41-44).

As I wrote this verse, I realized that I couldn't turn off the radio because I was identified with the web. I would get so caught up with the lyrics of the song that I would feel the pain of a breakup as if it were happening again in the moment. I would do this over and over and over again, as if putting myself through a torture chamber because one or two times wasn't sufficient enough. I now have the awareness to ask the question, "Is this happening now, or just in my mind?" The power in asking this question is that we get to shift and respond from choice.

That being said, what if our thoughts are instruments, and our mind is playing a song? If we attach to the words of the song as good, bad, sad, etc., then we attach to the story of the song and we create a reality based on the lyrics. The point isn't to stop the lyrics but to observe them. From present moment awareness, you simply observe your thoughts, feelings, emotions, past and/or future experiences without being swept by them.

The Monster

Have you ever gone out looking for an imagined monster? The search for it produces the same anxiety, fear, and desire to get away as a real monster would. You go hunting for it: you look behind doors or even under the bed. Everywhere you go, you are alert, aware, and in search of when that monster will show up next. It's as if that monster rules and runs your life, yet you never see it because it isn't there. This is the power of our minds when we attach to our thoughts as truth.

You see, we are conditioned to finding something wrong, so much so that, even when things are going well, we question whether or not that is normal. Because for many of us normal is, "Where is the monster?" I've also heard it as, "Waiting for the other shoe to drop," or "If everything is going good right now, something bad is bound to happen." It really doesn't matter what you call it. What matters is that you become aware of the complexity of the dis-ease that is created when we are identified with the web. This is why I chose to write this book—so that you can experience the essence of who and what we are.

Chains

In writing this, I am reminded of a story I have heard about baby elephants when they are held captive against their will. They are tied to a pole with a strong chain or rope, usually around their ankles. The baby elephants try to move, but they realize that they are chained. Although they are big, the pain they endure when they pull is too much for them to bear, so they give up.

The elephants grow bigger and stronger and eventually could walk away with the pole. But they don't because they are so used to being confined by the chain that they don't bother pulling. The chain is eventually removed, and although they are free to experience life without the chain, they remain in place as if still chained. This is exactly what happens with human beings. We are free, but we remain confined by our attachment to the web. This is a mental construct that doesn't allow us to experience the freedom that we are.

The Cage

I have lived most of my life creating barriers to protect myself from pain, as I felt people were pain creators. I spent most of my life trying to free myself from the cage, only to realize that the cage is a delusion that I created in my mind. I have often heard the saying, "You are the lock and the key," and I have come to know that no key is needed to free myself because I am already free.

Internal Observation

I have lived in an imaginary cage for years, thinking I needed to figure out how to get out so that I could fly, but there was no cage to free myself from to begin with. I was caught in a mental trap, and because I knew no other way, I went around in circles, trying to find my way out.

I was unaware that the only way out was in knowing and owning that I *am* free. I realized that if I live my life imagining that I need a key to free myself, I will continue to reach for a solution to a problem that isn't really there. I understand now that no key is needed because there was no lock to begin with. The only lock that was there was the lock that I attached to as truth.

YOU ARE THE LOCK AND THE KEY

Chapter 3

Hero-In

One day, as I pondered on what I wanted to teach in my coaching practice, I heard the word "heroin" come through in my mind. What I heard next was, "Heroin is one of the most addictive drugs in the world." Then I heard the word heroin split in two, so now it was "hero-in." And finally, the message that brought it all home for me: "If you try to find your Hero in anything other than God within you, you will always be lost."

Whoa, talk about perfection. The delusion of separateness stems from the imagination that God is separate from our very existence when God is one with all of creation.

The imagination that God is separate from us has kept many people in bondage because it keeps us from connecting to the hero that is available in us right now. I believe that alcohol, the most addictive legal drug, is called "spirit," and heroin, the most addictive drug split in two, is "hero-in" for a reason. Therefore, I ask you, "Where do you find Spirit or your Hero-In?" It is not just drugs that keep us reaching for the experience of God. Other examples of how we reach for God are through our relationships, money, achievements, etc. And in the midst of this, we lose sight of the God that is ever so present in the here and now.

WE ARE ONE WITH THE
FORCE THAT CREATED
US

Religion and Addiction

The following is a breakthrough I had that brought me to see how we separate ourselves from one another through the practice of religion. Which I believe was created to unite us, but that translation got lost somewhere in the shuffle. You see, when we attach our identity to the web, we are unable to see that we are whole. We see ourselves as separate from God and from one another. Therefore we use anything and everything to hurt each other, including God.

I remember having a conversation with one of my friends who happens to be a born-again Christian. This was a perfect experience for me to bring awareness to the pain that is created when we are identified with the web. My friend and I were on the phone speaking about spirituality, and at some point, he says, "I'm going to pray for you so that you can find God and make it into the Kingdom." I remember feeling confused because I knew there was an assumption in his statement that I hadn't found God. I also felt hurt and angry because I knew that type of statement had created many wars in the world.

A statement like that could only be made by someone attached to the web as their identity. I could see the attachment clearly because it screamed of, "If you do it the way that I'm doing it, which is the right way, then you will find God and make it into the Kingdom." This statement, in other words, says, "I've got the keys, and you don't, and the way to get the keys is by doing what I tell you because I found God and you haven't." This was just another lie exposed.

I don't believe any of us are separate from God, no matter what or who we believe God is. I also believe that convincing isn't necessary when we know the truth of who and what we are.

What's true for me is that I don't have to fit in because I don't see myself as separate from anyone. I also believe that anything that divides us isn't God and is the making of someone attached to the web as their identity.

That was just one of many experiences I've had with people who practice religion from their web. Hearing things such as, "Jesus is the only one true God," or "Jehovah is the only one true God," or "Allah is the only one true God." So on and so on. I have realized that, when religion is practiced this way, there is no room for anyone else's truth. We spend most of our time convincing, rather than being an example of God's love, no matter what we choose to call God.

GOD IS LOVE

Imagine

Imagine you were born into a family that practices a different religion than the one you grew up learning about. Imagine the religion you were taught is all you ever knew. You then go visit another country where they practice a different religion than you. The people of this country are going out of their way to convince you that the religion they practice is the truth and the way. Some would even say that believing anything different would result in death.

How would you feel?

I imagine you would feel confused, I know I would.

I share this because I know many people expect someone else to believe in the same God that they do. I believe it's beautiful to be passionate about the God we believe in. It is also important not to disregard what's true for someone else. What if what you were taught is not what they were taught, and what if you are the same as them? As in, we only know what we were taught to be true. How could you impose your truth on anyone else, and how could anyone else impose their truth on you? This does not mean that one should stop believing in the God that they believe in. It is to take inventory of where we may be suggesting that we are right and everyone else is wrong.

CHOOSE LOVE

There Is One God

I recall creating a music video for a song I wrote called "There Is One God." I decided to visit different temples so that I could capture images of people's faces. I wanted to capture what we all have in common, no matter what religion we practice.

I remember going to a Mosque and having a conversation with one of the men. We spoke about the 9/11 attacks, mostly because many Muslims were being judged as if all Muslims were the ones who committed those horrific acts.

I remember him passionately stating, "Those terrorists were not Muslim, Muslims do not kill." And I believe him. I feel sad that many of us put a whole group of people in a category because of our experiences with some.

I also recall having a conversation with a woman at a salon around the same time as the creation of my music video. She and I spoke about spirituality, and I shared that I was going away on a retreat. I told her that one of the things I loved most is the opportunity to be in silence and fasting for three days.

She then asked, "Is that a religious retreat? Because, in the religion I practice, we do something similar."

I responded, "No, it's not religious. It's spiritual," and then I asked curiously, "What religion do you practice?"

She paused, looked around the room, and then came closer to my ear, and whispered, "Don't tell anyone; I am Muslim."

At that moment, I felt sadness grow throughout my body, knowing that she felt afraid to share. My eyes filled with tears, and I said to her, "I feel so sad knowing you feel you have to whisper that."

She shared about experiences her friends and family had because they were Muslim, and I understood her concern.

After these experiences, I felt even more passion to share my song and music video. It was a humbling experience to spend time at a Buddhist temple, a Mandir, a Baptist church, a Mosque and a Catholic church. It was a true privilege to participate in rituals to celebrate God in ways I hadn't before. These are experiences I will not soon forget.

I SEE THE GOD IN ME,
THEREFORE I SEE THE
GOD IN YOU.

God Looks Just Like Us

There's a man by the name of Antoine Leiris who left a message for the terrorist who murdered his wife and many others due to different religious beliefs. The words he stated were so profound, deep, and true that I felt they had to be in my song. He said: "If the God for whom you kill so blindly made us in His image, each bullet in my wife's body would have been a wound in His heart."

That statement touched my heart because it is so true, and now I share with you the link to my song *There Is One God*: *https://youtu.be/AhC3n1Nq0FQ*

We are all the same. Seeing God in ourselves, as well as in each other, will free us from the wars that we create from our perception of perfection. I believe the opposite of God is conditional love, and that type of love comes from the conditioned mind. The mind that is conditioned to see, think and believe that our way is the best way and/or the only way. When there are many paths that take us to the same destination. I truly believe that these are the conversations that need to happen to bring awareness and healing to our world.

THERE ARE MANY PATHS
THAT LEAD US TO THE
SAME DESTINATION

Be as Loving as the God you believe in

It is both in our words and actions that we display God's love. To me, being an example of God's love is so powerful because it is our essence. I believe that God's love doesn't have to convince us because when we are fully aware that we are one with God, we are embodying truth by simply being who we are. I believe that God is a source of unconditional love, and that the point isn't to convince people that the true God is the one who we believe in, but to be as loving as the God we believe in, as an example of our devotion and truth.

A movie that I watched and admired greatly was *Hacksaw Ridge*. If you haven't watched it yet, I highly recommend that you do. In short, the movie is about a man who refused to use a gun in the war, as he was following one of the Ten Commandments: "Thou shall not kill." It is truly an incredible movie that offered me so much insight about faith and sanity. As I watched that movie, one of the things I realized was that most of us function through insanity.

By insanity, I mean the craziness of killing each other. Especially because I believe we are one; so, *as we hurt or kill someone else onto ourselves we are doing the same.* In my experience, the main character in the movie was the only sane one because he would not kill anyone, and even went so far as to help the enemy. As I watched the movie, the words I repeated in my mind were, "He is the only sane one," and I cried, knowing this is the truth.

I CHOOSE TO BE KIND
AND LOVING TOWARD
MYSELF AND OTHERS.

God's Hands

Here I will share an experience and conversation I had with God through meditation. I was emotionally moved to do my own open-heart surgery through meditation one day. So I went to my room, took my shirt and bra off, and laid down on my bed with a couple of pillows behind my back, elevating my chest. I then closed my eyes and put my fingertips toward the center of my chest and began to imagine myself pulling my chest open. I did this several times until I saw other hands begin to do my surgery for me. Although I didn't see a face, I knew, somehow, that it was God, and I was emotionally moved by the experience. I then heard God say, "I live in your heart."

With my eyes closed, I cried and said, "God, I give it all to you. Whatever you want, I will do."

God's response was, "I want you to love me more than anything and everything."

I responded with curiosity, "Yes and God, you said you live in my heart."

God answered, "Precisely; love yourself more than anything and everything."

In that very moment, I knew that when I love myself, I love God too, and how I love myself is how I love God because God and I are one.

LOVE YOURSELF MORE
THAN ANYTHING AND
EVERYTHING

Be Still and Know That I Am God

The difference between being powerless and powerful, is the difference between begging God to come to you and knowing that God is already here. I was taught as a child that I had to reach out and pray for God to come to me and that God will one day return. I watched many people desperately pray to God this way. I have realized throughout my journey that we are taught addictive behaviors through the imagination that God is separate from us.

Today, I am so grateful that I get to have the experience of God in every moment, which to me is the true ecstasy most of us live our lives seeking, and many of us die trying to find. I now believe that what we yearn for most is the experience of God that is here, now, and available for all of us. I believe we will experience a massive shift in our planet when we stop reaching out for something or someone to complete our sense of self, and I believe that happens when we fully know and own that we are whole, complete, and one with God.

Next, I will share another experience I had through meditation that helped deepen my awareness of the experience of God. I was speaking with Michael Cupo, author of a book that I highly recommend called *It's Monday Only In Your Mind*. One of the things he mentioned on our call was that when guiding people to meditate, he simply suggests that they go sit. He realized that when someone is told to meditate, they often have a preconceived notion of what meditation is supposed to look like, leaving people thinking about how to meditate, which defeats the purpose of meditation.

What he shared brought up some curiosity for me. So much so that after my conversation with him, I decided to go sit. I sat at the edge of my bed, closed my eyes, and shortly after, I heard the words, "Be still and know that I am God." I continued to sit and heard, "God is the stillness, and God can only be experienced in the stillness of our minds."

This message was very clear and beautiful. God is the experience I have when I'm simply here, meeting life where it is. Right here, right now, there's no other place to be. I genuinely believe that each time we reach out for an experience, a high if you will, through alcohol, drugs, a person or experience, what we are really reaching for is God outside of ourselves, which means we forgot that God is present in our hearts right now.

GOD IS THE STILLNESS,
AND GOD COULD ONLY
BE EXPERIENCED IN THE
STILLNESS OF OUR
MINDS

We Are Cells in One Body

I recently had a vision of all humankind as cells in one body. This was pretty incredible, especially because I understood that this is what we truly are. As I observed the cells, I saw that some cells had forgotten that they are cells. Still others had remembered, and they wanted everyone to know that they are a cell, too (this cell is totally me). I love what I have been unveiling and that I get to share it with you. I love that by discovering myself, I get to direct you to a place in yourself where you have access to absolutely everything. You are everything and everyone on the planet. In fact, you are the planet; you are the entire universe in a body.

I know that many people are aware of this. You might be one of them and if you are, you are a change maker. You are helping people become aware of their power and the world is better because you decided to share your light. If this concept is new to you, you are beginning to get it and you may be excited about what's possible. I'm excited for you, wherever you may be on your journey. I'm excited that you are here reading this book, expanding your mind and heart.

WE ARE ONE

Chapter 4

Masculine and Feminine Forces

The masculine force is that of doing, and the feminine force is that of being. In landing in my heart and going through the ultimate internal shift, I understand that having one without the other is like death. Death, because we will be functioning like zombies in the world, ego-driven, with no true direction. That is how most of the world has been and is functioning now. The forces of our energy are mostly directed outward, fighting to win a battle that isn't out there. The battle is between the masculine and feminine forces within, as they face away from each other and fight to meet and greet one another in love.

You see, most of us were taught that there is a "better than" or "less than" stance in the world. That teaching says that masculine is better than feminine, and we are mostly driven by believing that this is true. We have attached to a system that has not and will not work. This way has created more separation in the world than can be fathomed by the heart. Most of us are trying to escape pain, and we are going about it the wrong way. It is an inside journey. A journey full of exploration and observation, simply to experience the rapture of what it really feels like to be alive.

Victory

If your victory is determined by the goals you meet or the things you attain, then you are lost in reaching for the experience that you already are. There are so many of us that determine our victory as a filler to our identity. A filler means we are functioning from empty, trying to be filled by external things because we forgot that we are the things we want and desire.

This is not to say we shouldn't go toward our goals or celebrate our achievements, but to observe where our desires come from. Do they come from a place of despair and desire to be seen as worthy, or do they come from a place of choice and knowing that you were born worthy? I am aware that when I am identified with my thoughts, I am of the imagination that I have to have certain things to meet my identified version of victory. A version that isn't the best version of me and I know that I am not alone in this.

I really got it when I observed commercials for the next-level iPhone, how so many people would go crazy to get it. Then, shortly after, another iPhone with some new features would be created, and people would go crazy over getting that one, and so on and so on. I am aware that some people simply like luxury of all kinds, so it's not to deem luxury bad or wrong because it's not. It is to bring awareness to those that attach to the idea that they need luxury or a degree to be worthy. Many of us even go to school to fulfill an identity that says, "I am worthy when I am successful," when in fact we are worthy simply because we are alive.

As I mentioned earlier, this is not to say you shouldn't buy the things you want or shouldn't get an education, but to observe where your desires come from. I realize that I can purchase something to fill a void, or I can purchase something knowing that I am enough, with or without the things I have. The same goes for my education. I can achieve my master's to prove that I am a master, or I can achieve my master's knowing that I am one, and from this knowing, I can choose this path, never needing to prove that I could.

Joy

What I have recognized is that, quite often, people assume that someone who has a certain car, a particular house or profession is happier than someone who doesn't. Which isn't necessarily true. In reflecting on this, I gave some thought to the following questions.

What creates true joy? Is it things? A house, a car, a pool? What about achievements; the degree, the goal, the race? Competing, achieving, winning? Or is it the perfect relationship? Marriage and babies?

Then I thought, "What if all of those things are a part of our joy, but not the reason for our joy? What if all of our experiences are reflections of what we are?"

Many of us live our lives chasing the experience of joy, bliss and ecstasy. Unaware that chasing those experiences takes us further away from what we really want because what we really want is what we already are. Therefore, we lose sight of ourselves and our true power by chasing our own reflection.

As I sit here and write, I can't help but think about the many famous people who have committed suicide. This is not just by literally killing themselves, but also by doing things that leave them feeling disconnected and further away from their true self.

Many people ask, "What happened to those people? What steered them so far away from themselves?"

I will not claim to know what the answers are for them, but this confirms that joy isn't about what we have. If we attach to the web of "I'll feel joy when I get there or have that." Then we will arrive at our perceived joy location, only to produce a temporary joy. With temporary joy comes the need for another and another. When we remember that we are joy, then we celebrate everything with joy, simply because we are alive to experience it. It is then that life becomes a joyous experience, a celebration of everything; A celebration of YOU!

You Are Now

There have been times in my life when I wanted to get to the present moment. As if the moment was a destination that I would arrive at some future point. I have said and heard things such as,

"Come back into the now," or "Return to the present". Although those statements were created to bring awareness, I could see how they can be misleading if not stated properly.

As I listened to those statements, I imagined that I must do something to arrive at the moment. This is another form of bondage because it will have us living in insanity, trying to get somewhere, simply to realize that the place we have been trying to arrive at is right where we are. This is what we do for many things in life: we wait to arrive to be happy, whole, complete, loved, and more.

I chased the moment so much that I lost myself trying to find it. I also did this with achievements, goals, wants, desires, and more. I was addicted to working hard to get somewhere and achieve something, not knowing that I was yearning to be right where I am, achieving the love of me.

I was lost in continuously reaching for the next best thing. As I write that, I realize that the underlying message is that the best thing isn't me right here, right now. That notion can only keep me addicted to getting better, as if I am not good enough now. I have become aware of how crazy it is to live this way.

Living this way is overlooking the beauty and privilege of the breath, the heartbeat, and the soul of everything. Living this way is never being grateful for what is. Living this way is forgetting how precious, beautiful, and miraculous life is just as it is right now. We miss out on the beauty that exists in every precious moment when we chase the moment as a destination. That being said, know that you arrived a long time ago. Accept that you are here, look around, see the beauty that surrounds you and see the beauty that is you. You are home.

Be Yourself

I read somewhere the phrase, "Be yourself," and I thought, "How does someone know how to be themselves, if, for a lifetime, they have been taught to be something or someone they're really not, and how does someone know that this is so?"

Through my inner journey, I saw all the abstract colors of choices I had made in the past according to who I was told I should be, or what I should be like in order to be liked or even loved. At a very young age, my focus was mostly on other people's perception of me. I was on an outside-in journey, unaware that I was going the "wrong direction."

I quoted "wrong direction" because the wrong direction was the right direction for me to become who I am, so that I could take a stand for what I do. I stand for LOVE, as me and as you, as us, as one, whole and complete, and I am beyond grateful that you are on this journey with me. Being myself has become something entirely different than what I was told and imagined.

Being myself is an extension of my connection with the Divine Spirit in service to the greater good of humanity. A love that goes on lifetime after lifetime, not having to prove itself and knowing that being itself is more than enough. I am more than enough; I am fluidity from the hardest working muscle in my body—my heart. Words can't express the freedom that many people, including myself, have experienced as they have taken off the veils of imperfection to see how truly perfect, we all are. If you have not yet experienced it, this is the time for you.

You Are Not Your Masks

As you unmask layer upon layer of what you have imagined your identity to be, you will begin to experience truth on a whole different dimension. I learned through my healing journey that I created tons of masks. I often joke that I was brought to the mask store when I was younger and said, "I'll take all the masks you've got."

Living protected, defended, and confused with no direction, only to find that I was creating the suffering that I imagined was happening to me. A life full of suffering is a life of a lost identity. A life of peace is becoming aware of how powerful we truly are in every moment, as we remember that we are free, here and now. So, if you haven't already done so, take a look and see the protective masks you've created, and take them off one by one until you stand naked in your truth.

This I know for sure: you are so much more than the barriers you created to protect yourself from pain. You are the light of love that shines from within you. You are the fire in your eyes. You were born with inherent worth, and I know that simply because you are here. No other evidence is necessary, you are living proof that miracles exist.

Love is Not a Feeling

A friend of mine, Love Coach Catherine Danieli, shared this statement on social media: "Love is Not a Feeling," and I couldn't agree more. When we are attached to love as a feeling, we chase whatever the feeling is until we get it, and when that feeling goes away, we yearn for it again, and again, and again. This is what creates an addictive pattern because we will not be satisfied until we experience love as the identified feeling.

When we remember that love is our true essence, we stop reaching for love externally. And even when we do reach out for it, we can take a breath, put our hand on our own heart, and know that we are home, in love with ourselves.

I have shared all of these attachments and ways that we allow ourselves to be led by illusions so that you are able to be present and aware as you continue to read. I know you are ready; let's continue to go deeper.

Chapter 5

Behind the Mirror

I recall an experience I had as I looked in the mirror while lying in bed one day. At some point, I reached behind the mirror to grab a pillow, but the pillow I saw was in the mirror. I realized that was an illusion because what I went to grab wasn't behind the mirror, it was inside. In that moment, I understood that the mirror is my only true reality because the mirror is me. So, when I go out to grab something that I see in the mirror, I am of the imagination that what I see is out there when it really isn't.

That experience provided me with an understanding of what it is I do when I attach to an imagined reality. I am aware that, when I am projecting, I am grabbing something behind the mirror that isn't really there. I am attaching to the imagination that what I see in the mirror is something that I can grab, yet the mirror is a reflection of me.

I've come to realize that everyone is a mirror for me to see my own reflection, and I believe I am a mirror for everyone too. I have asked people to look into my eyes and tell me who they see. Most people say, "I see myself." My response to that is, "Yes, and when I look into your eyes, I see myself too because you are a mirror of me, and I am a mirror of you."

I've learned that what we like or dislike in another person or people is often not about them. It's about the things we've disowned about ourselves. The beauty of this awareness is that when the glitch that has us grab something behind the mirror lessens, we regain our power. We see ourselves clearer and we are able to make choices from the love that we are. We are able to stay in our power and from our power we remind people of theirs.

EVERYONE ON THIS
PLANET IS A MIRROR
FOR US TO SEE OUR
REFLECTION

Projection

I was at a stoplight, waiting for the light to change and I saw a man standing on the sidewalk. Although I couldn't hear him, I could tell that he was having an intense argument. Nobody was in front of him but he was pointing and yelling as if there was. I observed him for a while until he completed his fight by spitting, sticking out his middle finger, and then turning around and stomping away.

The thought that came through for me after that experience was, "We can call him crazy because he's yelling at the air, but we do the same thing when we yell or fight against another person. We just call ourselves sane because we have a visible screen. But we are no different than that man when we are attacking another person".

I realized how truly abusive it is to imagine ourselves as separate from each other, not only for the other person but for our own soul as well. Many of us live this way, in reaction to everything and everyone.

Some will say but they did XYZ. Which means we are looking for something to justify our behavior. Rather than being fully accountable for our own. It has helped me to see that other people's reactions toward me have little to do with me. They are a mirror for me, and I am a mirror for them too. Unaware of this, we yell and fight about who's right and who's wrong but that only takes us so far.

It's just like being provided with feedback that may feel as if someone is punching you, and I ask that you imagine their fist up toward you. Then you react to the feedback and put your fist up too. So now there are two fists going head-to-head and going nowhere. Now imagine yourself with your palm open, receiving the feedback. Shifting the way that you respond, especially when it feels difficult.

"DARKNESS CANNOT DRIVE OUT DARKNESS; ONLY LIGHT CAN DO THAT. HATE CANNOT DRIVE OUT HATE; ONLY LOVE CAN DO THAT."

Dr. Martin Luther King Jr.

We bite too

I was at a park taking a walk with my dog, Lola, when I noticed some people were trying to pass us. One woman stopped and asked, "Does your dog bite?" I said, "No, she's a sweet girl." Then a man that was about to pass us overheard our conversation and stated, "of course she bites she's a dog". I then responded, and so do humans.

I realized after that statement that we do bite, not just with our teeth but with our words too. We make judgments according to our perception of perfection. We categorize people and animals too. Many people have seen my dog and they're terrified because they are afraid of pitbulls. "Those dogs attack people". No, some dogs have but not all of them are the same. Just like no human is the same. This is what we do. We say things like, "Muslims are bad" "Black people are bad" "White people are bad" "Hispanics are bad" "The cops are bad" "All men are bad" "All women are bad"

We categorize people and then wonder why there are wars in the world.

We are all one and we are all unique. We all have our own unique handprints. A print that can open doors only meant for us. No one else can open the doors that were made to be opened by your handprint.

We categorize ourselves and others and we create limitations according to our beliefs. We weren't meant to be categorized.

Categorization creates separation and this separation keeps us in bondage. It is said that the only way out is through, and I say that the only way out is IN, inside of you. Turn inward if you haven't already. Get to know the uniqueness of your being. It is then that you will see and accept other people's uniqueness too.

WE ARE ALL ONE AND WE
ARE ALL UNIQUE

Reflection

I recall an observation I made when I saw my dog, looking at herself in the mirror. I remember when she was a baby, she would look at herself and lick the mirror; it was the cutest thing. Then months passed, she got older and spent little to no time in front of a mirror.

One day, I decided to put a big mirror in the kitchen where she spent most of her time. I observed her reaction as she saw herself. She would bark, and in my imagination, she was asking, "Who is that, and what is she doing here?" She would jump around the same way she would if there were another dog in the room.

I found that experience to be so interesting. As I observed her I thought: if all she sees is human beings around her, she may imagine that her reflection looks like theirs. Then I took that in for myself and thought, "If what I see most are other people, I too will begin to imagine I am who I see, and I will be less identified with the reflection of me."

The mirror that we offer to one another is our eyes so that we can reflect and know that all we see in the world is ourselves. These many mirrors tell a great deal of the importance of being aware of the world that resides within us. They are also opportunities to see ourselves as we are, whole and complete.

After I reflected on my experience with my dog and the mirror, I had a conversation with a friend. She said she hated taking pictures because she saw herself as ugly. She told me, "A lot has changed since I had my stroke, and I don't look the way I used to."

The question I posed to her was, "If I were in your shoes, would you look at me and say, 'You shouldn't take a picture because you don't look the way you used to?'" She looked at me and said, "Of course not!"

I asked, "So then why would you treat me better than you treat yourself?"

She was a woman of faith, and she began to share about how God made us in his image, and I said, "That's right; so, every time you state, "You are ugly" to yourself, you are stating that about God because God is one with you."

If you can relate to negative self-talk, know that you are the most important person in your life, and how you treat yourself matters. What I got from watching my dog is the fact that we see other people more than we see ourselves; therefore, we begin to imagine that we are who we see most, when, in reality, we are who we are with most, which is ourselves.

A practice that I started years ago and is one of the most important things that I offer myself often, is what I call "mirror love." I look in the mirror, close enough to see my reflection in my eyes, and I speak words of love to myself. This can be a very emotional practice, especially if you haven't done it or if you don't do it often. That being said, I recommend that you begin to share kind and loving words to the one you see in the mirror. Even if you have to start slowly by finding one thing you like or stating, "I am working on loving you as you are, and I will take steps to do so every single day because you matter to me," it doesn't really matter how you start. What truly matters is that you do.

Also, for those who are unable to see themselves fully and who struggle with self-love, take the time to touch your face and state as you touch your nose, "I love my nose." If you are unable to do that, begin to see a mirror of yourself in your imagination, and speak love unto yourself in whatever way you choose. This exercise is for everyone. Let's strengthen and grow the love revolution by starting with the man or woman in the mirror. As you grow in love, begin to share your love with those who don't know how or are struggling with loving themselves. Do this by being an example of what it looks like to embody the love that you are. Know that when you do, you create opportunities for other people to learn how to embody love too.

BE EXTRA LOVING TO
THE ONE YOU ARE WITH
MOST.

I Found Love

There's a song called "I Still Haven't Found What I'm Looking For" by U2, and I can relate to those words. I spent most of my life trying to find what I was looking for, until the day I knew my search was over because I finally found the love of me.

In October 2008, I went to a two-week conference called Heart, created by Carole Kammen, founder of Pathways Institute—a school devoted to the exploration of human consciousness.

Going to my first two-week conference was a bit challenging for me. I had to leave my son for two weeks for the very first time. I had to invest money, and I had to face the many judgments that people had of me because I was leaving my son for twelve days. But somehow, I just knew I had to go, so I did.

I took a flight to Arizona and spent twelve days isolated with no internet, no television, no phone, no way to connect with the outside world. I knew that would be a challenge, and I found out shortly after that it was completely necessary to disconnect to better connect to myself.

I remember one night, right before bed: I asked for a dream that would deepen my connection to my heart. I had my own room, and there was no outside lighting except for the beautiful stars. I fell asleep, and at about two in the morning, I woke up startled. I heard a woman's voice in my room saying my name, "Loida." The voice was loud, and it was dark in my room.

I turned on the light nervously, not knowing who or what I would see. I looked around the room, and nobody else was there. I then looked at my hand and started to cry. As I touched and admired my hand, I said aloud, "I have been waiting for this moment for so long," and I cried. I tear up as I write because that moment was so profound for me.

I had to shut out all of the outside noise to hear the voice of my heart. I remember getting out of bed, going to the bathroom mirror, and crying. I felt as if I was seeing myself for the very first time. After that conference, I came home and wrote and recorded "I Found Love" *(https://youtu.be/24PGXMqkzxw)*.

Behind the Mirror

The lyrics are:

So much time I spent trying to find myself outside myself, trying to grasp the love I could not get from no one else, but I found it within me internal love is where I want to be.

Oh, so sweet, when I'm loving me unconditionally. Oh yeah, I found love, I found love, so sweet, inside of me, inside of me.

I searched in books, in people's advice, sometimes I felt like my life was the price, oh, oh, oh, oh. A temporary fix, I'm sick of it, I don't want it, no, no, no. I'm breaking off these chains, the same I will not stay, I found me a better way, oh, oh, oh. It's right here in my chest, I'm feeling so blessed, I found true happiness.

Oh, so sweet when I'm loving me unconditionally. Oh yeah, I found love, I found love, so sweet, inside of me, inside of me.

I never felt quite like this before, when I look into my eyes there's a love so pure; thought I needed a fix, but I found a cure, the love I sought was mine and now I soar.

Oh, so sweet when I'm loving me unconditionally. Oh yeah, I found love, I found love so sweet, inside of me, inside of me. I found looove…

IT IS SO REFRESHING TO
LOVE MYSELF THIS WAY,
AND I LOVE THAT I GET
TO GUIDE YOU TO SEE,
FEEL AND EXPERIENCE
THE GREATEST LOVE OF
ALL INSIDE OF YOU

Go and Be Liberated

Is there something that you are holding on to that may be keeping you stuck? Are there beliefs or patterns that you have not released that are not serving you anymore? Are you living as the joyous child that you are, or do you have your adult hat on all the time, screaming, "This is how things should be," with no flexibility? And is that how you want to live? Or do you want to be liberated from the imagination that life should look or be a certain way for you to be happy?

If you want to be liberated, follow me to the last part of my book. Some of the following will sound familiar from what you have previously read and know that I am taking you deeper into the journey to where you will see and experience how truly remarkable you are. I can't wait for you to see, feel, and experience the transformation that happens when you remember that you were born a winner. Come join me. Let go and let's go.

FREEDOM AWAITS YOU

Chapter 6

Awaken

I recall the day and situation in which I saw the deceit of the perceived loser that needed to win. I realized that I was doing all of this in my mind, yet I had an external experience of it and the lie was revealed.

I was driving and came upon a two-lane road that merged into a one-lane to get onto the highway. When I got onto the two-lane road, there was another car next to me. I sped up to get to the one-lane first, and then the person next to me sped up and I decided to let them go first. I saw that if I had sped up more, they would have sped up more, and in doing so, we would have both been fighting to win. Then, right before I let them go ahead, the thought that crossed my mind was, "If I already won, would I still want to speed to win?" The answer was no, because I wouldn't have to. I would know and own what I already won.

I was then able to see this pattern play out in so many ways. I would create a race to win in my mind and when I "lost" I would feel depleted and unworthy. When truth be told the only thing that I lost was myself in an imagination.

I was living a life of "I will prove I can", from a mind that was attached to losing. Distortion after distortion, when we are unaware, that is what we get caught up in. Then we create realities according to lies. I saw this more and more as I meditated, quieting my mind and bringing my awareness to the present moment.

As I meditated, I observed what I would do with my thoughts. I noticed when I'd go for an unnecessary ride of sadness. At times I would imagine how I would feel if someone in my family passed away. I would literally allow my thoughts to take me all the way to their wake and I would cry and experience grief from just a thought. I would get on a thought train and I would allow my thoughts to take me for a ride. A ride that I didn't want to be on and without awareness I had no choice.

I'd get caught like a hamster on its wheel, going round and round and round—that's what we do when we aren't aware. We get a thought and then we attach to it and we create a reality according to our thoughts.

This does not mean that our thoughts are the enemy because they're not. However, many of us are attached to a negative way of thinking because that's all we heard. How could we know anything different?

You are here though reading this book and possibly becoming aware for the very first time that you have a choice. As you become more aware of your attachment to the web, you experience freedom. You get to walk on the web and create more of what you desire with it.

The experience of spiraling negative thoughts comes from a lost identity. When we are identified with the web, we aren't aware that we have a choice at all. The work then becomes to see our true self as the spider that created the web. The spider is able to walk around the web and has more web to spin what it desires. You can stay stuck identifying with the web or you can choose to see that you are the creator. One will keep you feeling imprisoned in your mind. The other will allow you to experience the freedom that you are. What will you choose?

You Have Nothing to Prove

This is a statement I made to some young boys I saw fighting in the street. I said, "When you fight, you have something to prove; you think your worth is based on you winning or being right, when the truth is, you don't have to prove yourself". This is a masked identity that has held many people hostage in their lives. I must beautify, I must perfect, I must win to be happy. Keeping many trapped in a future projection of winning.

When we are identified with the web we are lost, therefore everything becomes a competition. Mostly because from this attachment we are trying to make our way back home to ourselves.

We become addicted to our thoughts and end up feeling like we are going crazy. This is why meditation is such a powerful tool. It gives us an opportunity to observe our thoughts without attaching a reality to them. It also gives us the opportunity to be present with all of the feelings that come up for us as we think about something. The more we practice meditation the more we become aware that the power we seek is in the moment.

When we are attached to the web, even the moment becomes a goal. We are racing most, if not all of the time. Racing in our mind, racing to get somewhere, racing to achieve, etc. This is no different than being addicted to a drug.

That being said, have you ever felt like an addict of your mind? For example, your mind is racing, and you don't know what to do, but you want to fix it or make it stop. You are fixated on trying to figure something out or fix it somehow? Whether you have felt like an addict of your mind, or currently do, know that you are the spider. That you have the power to observe the web and see it for what it is. Therefore, you can stop spinning if you desire. You have the power to walk on the web and you have the power to create a new one. Begin to create webs that serve you to feel joyful, blissful, happy and connected to all things. A web that fulfills your heart's desires.

When I was identified with the web, anxiety became oh so familiar. Then I realized that I wanted to win despair and anxiety too. I was living in an imaginary race all of the time. But then again aren't most of us? I personally believe we got the words human race confused. Because that's what many of us have been, humans racing to win. As we become aware of this, we get to slow down and we get to enjoy the journey.

When we are identified with the web, we are not enjoying the journey. We are either trying to figure out how to get out of the web or we are so attached to it that we go out of our way to prove that it's the truth. We are either better than or less than. Which means we either won the outer race or we lost it. From this place in ourselves, we can only experience intense highs and intense lows, versus living in balance. An opportunity to live a balanced life is what I am offering you here, as you begin to live and embody the winner in you.

This winner does not arise from any outer achievement, but from the very existence that you are. This winner does not scream, "Haha, I won, and you didn't." This winner knows we all won, for we all went through the same journey. This winner sees everyone as whole and complete, and as one with God, no matter what. This winner experiences joy at its maximum capacity because this winner is filled with gratitude for EVERYTHING!

Awareness

The awareness of attachment has been such a gift. There are so many things that have been revealed to me. I now have a clear choice on how to respond and where from. I realize that everything that wasn't working in my life was due to my relationship to it—losing or winning. For example, I've had the same relationship with money. Those times when I had a lot, I thought to myself that I was winning, and when I didn't have any, I fell in despair because I thought I had lost. Yet the only thing I had lost was myself in an illusion.

I was left feeling defeated, battered, and bruised because I was so identified with the loss of money as the loss of myself. I gave all of my power away to a fight I didn't even know I was fighting. The fight that I was in was that of wanting to win from a false identity. As a result, my perception of self was that of being a loser that had to win to be okay. Well, that was a lie. All of it was an illusion of winning and defeat. We are only winning or losing from our man-made perspective of what it means to win or lose.

Another example of the relationship I had with winning and losing is the battle I had with time. Time is something I have always fought to win—racing to be on time and just making it, or ugh, I lost, I'm late, eventually accepting defeat. As I write these things down, I am in awe, and I also laugh at the craziness I've put myself through, as I have fought to win a "battle" that I've already won.

That even being lost in time became a loss of awareness.

I realized that trying to hold on to time is like trying to hold water in your hand with a clenched fist: it seeps through and eventually disappears. Time does not wait for us, nor is time something we race to catch. If you try to catch 1 p.m., you may catch it, but only for one second. For soon thereafter that minute will be followed by 1 second, then 2 seconds and so on. Time is not meant to be caught; moments are meant to be experienced. Yet we give time so much control over our lives. Why? Why do we do this when time is an illusion?

"I don't have time for this," "I don't have time for that," "I'm going to be late," "I'm right on time." Our relationship with time mostly controls us, it's either working with us or against us. Yet, what if I am time and time is me and what if the same applies to money and all of the things we desire? What then? If those things are that powerful, then where does the power go when we release the illusion of them, and take it all in? The power goes to the rightful owner: me, you, we, us.

I See You

The Awakened Winners

There are so many ways in which to prove that we won externally. I personally spent a lot of my life trying to conquer my fears, as in winning them. I have realized that, if I'm of the notion that I have lost and need to win, I'm always going to want to conquer my fears. If that's what I do, then what I will always do is fight to conquer an illusion, a lie.

We get caught up in lies when we are unaware. These are lies that are revealed through silence. Lies that I chose to strongly discipline myself to hear through meditation.

I remember yet another experience I had through meditation that is too profound not to share. I remember sitting, closing my eyes and immediately seeing myself. Yet, the self that I saw had an open space on her chest, like a missing piece of skin. I saw her reaching for things externally, money, relationships, education, etc. She then would put what she grabbed on the empty space of her chest, and the empty space would disappear. Then suddenly a new empty space appeared somewhere else on her body, and she would grab something else. She'd fill the void with that, and on and on she went. Shortly after, I saw another self-appear in that same meditation. So there were two of me. I realized that the second self served as a witness to the self that was filling the void. It did not try to stop or distract in any way, it simply witnessed. I realized that is my true self, the part of me that can simply witness all of the lies without attachment. This was a powerful meditation; it allowed me the privilege of seeing attachment on a whole different level.

The witness function is no different than the spider point of view. From the spider point of view, we get to witness the web. From the web point of view we are in doubt of the truth that we are winners, therefore there's never enough. No workshop is enough, no book is enough, no person, no place, nothing is ever enough. I was so caught in a false identity that I'd go around trying hard to figure it all out, only to find that I was searching for myself all along. To this, I say, release the need to understand. The truth of who you are is whole, complete, and all-knowing; you are wisdom and the wisdom that you are knows way more than what you imagine you need to know from a false identity. So remember who you are and say out loud, "I've got this, I'm driving now."

Breaking

The thought of breaking has a bad rep, but what if breaking is a gift? Allowing ourselves to fall so that we can see IN through the cracks? I used to want to control just so that I wouldn't fall because I was afraid that if I did, I would never come back from the fall. Then I tried this thing called falling, over and over and over again. The more that I fell, the more that I broke, until I could see that the "I" that I was identified with wasn't really me. It was a false identity, full of false beliefs and false wisdom that did not serve me to be all that I am.

So breaking became a gift, a gift of seeing and believing in something so much bigger than the "I" that I was identified with.

This breaking allowed me to see my true self. The self that doesn't attach to anything and is present with everything, moment by moment. A present moment existence that allows me the privilege of celebrating all of life and all parts of me unconditionally.

It is a humbling experience and a gift to know myself this way. I'm no longer afraid to break because breaking helps me see, and I can see the web clearly. My prayer is that you can too. Remember your power is in seeing yourself as the spider that creates it all. You are magic and you are connected to depths beyond your imagination. You are a God and a Goddess. A beautiful being of energy, source and matter. You are magnificent just as you are.

Chapter 7

We Already Won

Winning was never a future thing for me, for you, or for us—it was an illusion, a place where we could only see all our losses or all of our gains from an external point of view. I would experience all my losses in the past and feel all my wins in the future. My experience was that when my wins came, they were temporary; a temporary fix for someone attached to the web as their identity.

My temporary wins would create more ways to win to experience a high that comes from external validation. Now I know the truth because I learned to love, celebrate, and see myself. I now know that I am the high that I was seeking. I am the ecstasy and the joy I sought. I love that I decided to turn inward for true love and that in doing so I found that I was whole all along.

In this lifetime we get to co-create with God and the Goddess within us. When we attach to the imagination that we are separate from God and the Goddess, we lose sight of our inherent power. Many of us are attached to the identity of the loser and we go out of our way to win out there. It's a see me, love me, accept me point of view. Not knowing that our deep desire is to see, love and accept ourselves. It is then that we can begin to investigate the stories we attach to and it is then that we can create the life that we desire. A beautiful and magical co-creation with God and the Goddess within.

Destined

We are destined to win or destined to fail are both stories we attach to. Either we are chasing a reality we want, or we are sitting in self-loathing of where we are. There will be ample stories to prove our reality. Examples are, "I try and I always end up losing," "I give my all, and it's never enough," "I conquer everything I go for," or "I race and win first place all the time."

When I think of the word "destined," I think of the word "destiny," which is a location in the future we are destined to be. If I attach to the imagination that I am my destiny, my reality will be equated with that of reaching for something in the future, rather than fully being in the destination of now. Now is the true experience of winning from a heart-centered place.

Now keeps us present and aware of the complex, without attaching to our complex as our reality. When we truly awaken, we become aware of the illusion of destiny, and we remember that we are destined to be right where we are. From here, there's so much choice on how to move forward and what direction to go. I want to go this way; I want to go that way; we take deliberate steps toward the direction that our heart desires; this is freedom.

I don't have to work hard to win if I already won. If I perceive myself as a loser, then my life's work will be to win in all areas of my life. Therefore, creating the losing external battle because I have to be losing to be fighting to win. The goal is to know and own that I already won. It is then that I can drop all of the war masks and personas of determination and just be here as the winner that I am.

Now here it is, the moment you've been waiting for. Watch the journey you went on before you were born: We Already Won. *https://youtu.be/a4LoZlYaBEA*

Did you watch it? Did you see that you won before you were born? If so, I am excited that you know that you were born a winner and that you are both the sperm and the egg; therefore, you were born whole. You don't need anyone to complete you because you are already complete. Own the beauty of your existence; you are magnificent simply because you are alive. Rejoice in that truth. You are a winner!

What has been your attachment "drug" of choice (and I quote "drug" because the drug doesn't have to be literal)? It could be anything you attach your identity to. When entangled in the web your desire may be to fix or get fixed. For me, it was getting fixed. I was literally fixated on fixing myself because I imagined myself to be broken, unworthy, and unlovable.

We Already Won

I would attach to my past as a loser and the future as a winner. I would get trapped thinking about the past, imagining how it should have been or I would focus on the future from despair and need.

Perceiving my past as a loser and my future as a winner had me experiencing losing in every area of my life in the past and striving to win in the future. This made my life a constant battle.

I either worked my butt off to prove I had inherent worth, or I chucked the finger at the world and said "I don't need you." Both ways eventually left me feeling alone, confused, and afraid. I realized that when I attach to the web I create a fight and then I fight myself. When we are entangled in the web that is all we can do because we are trying to find our way out of it. It is a never-ending battle but the battle is you against you. There's freedom in remembering that you are the spider that created the web and that you are the sperm that got to the egg. You already won.

I've worked long and hard to win, and today, I'm so glad to know the truth. I now let go and experience the freedom that is always here.

I am grateful for the ability to notice where I am in myself when I think about something. For example, when I think to myself, "Wow, great, I had no anxiety today." I'm functioning from an external winner-loser mentality. At that moment, I'm referencing the past loser and stating that I conquered my past in the present; therefore I am not truly present with what is, I'm present with what was. In this way I am creating a false winning experience to fulfill a false identity. It is a lie conquering a lie; but now I know the truth. I know that when I am identified with the web, I experience dis-ease of the mind. When I am all in my mind, I am out of alignment with the truth of who and what I am in each moment.

I am a winner, not because I won some external battle. I am a winner because I won before I was born. I was born a winner, and because of that, I no longer have to go out of my way to prove myself, I can just be here like the winner that I am.

That being said, notice when you reference the past in the present, as in, "I'm better than I was before." When you do that, you are out of alignment with the present moment and where you are now, not yesterday, not tomorrow, now. I LOVE that I just noticed that NOW backward spells WON because you already WON, right here and right NOW. What is better than this moment? Nothing—it is when we are attached to the delusion of the mind that we imagine that better is a rearranging of the past or destination of the future, which will keep us imprisoned because the journey is not back or forth, it is right here where we are.

The beauty of the moment is that we never go away from it; the moment is always here and so are we. The thought of getting in the moment is making the moment a future goal, which is arbitrary to the concept and truth that we are already here, now. You have always been and always will be. Imagining anything other than that is your attachment to a false identity. When, truth be told, we are this moment.

To this I say, stop future tripping and start thinking, living, and speaking as if what you know will happen has already happened. Such as, "This book will be amazing," no—"This book is AMAZING RIGHT NOW, TODAY, because I ALREADY WON." This way, you can change your default channel from loser to WINNER. You already won. Don't doubt it; feel it with every part of your being because it is true. You already won. Maybe you thought you were losing, or you thought you had lost because you were lost in an imagination and called it truth. Those were just delusions, lies that you were attached to, from a man-made idea that you have to achieve something to win. Well, you don't have to work so hard anymore because you already won.

"Oh, but this feels untrue because—" No, no, STOP. That is the you that you thought you were, but you now know the truth. You already won; therefore, you don't have to fight to win.

"What do I do then?" You ask from the web.

Here's what you do: You celebrate every moment because you already won. You celebrate the fact that you're alive because you already won. You celebrate that you exist because you already won. There's no war to fight because you already won. You were born with inherent worth. You were born a winner, and at some point, you were misguided. People who were identified with their web told you differently. You were possibly attached to a message you heard somewhere, or you had an experience or set of experiences in which you felt torn down. No matter what the case was, that never changed what's true: you have been a winner since before day one. YOU WERE BORN A WINNER; therefore, you don't have to fight to win because YOU ALREADY WON.

You now speak, talk, live and love like the winner that you are and always have been. There's nothing you need to change about yourself because you already won.

You know and own that you already won—not as in, "I won against others," or, "I won this game," etc., but by owning that you were the sperm that made it to the egg. That you went on a journey before you were born and you arrived here, you won. Say it to yourself over and over again, "I already won; I was born a winner and I have been a winner since before day one because I fought long and hard to be born. The moment that the sperm met the egg, I won".

There's nothing more valuable than this truth; there's nothing else you need to know or do because you already won. This doesn't mean you don't create, and that you lay down in bed every day until you die. It means that you are doing things when you choose to do them from your heart and from the knowing that you were born with inherent worth.

This awareness is everything. You get to play and enjoy life simply because you exist. You made it. You have fought the "I have to prove myself" battle for long enough. Now you are able to see from the true you. You have taken off the veils of lies and all that is left is the knowing that you already won.

I want you to know that it's okay to cry, as you may have realized a truth that you weren't aware of and that it may be a difficult concept to grasp quickly. Take some time to grieve if you want to, but don't stay there feeling defeated because you're not. You are a winner. You already won. That is something to celebrate every second of the day.

You were a winner before you were born, you were born with inherent worth, you were born worthy, you are love, you are light, you are beautiful, you are miraculous, and you already won. These are not future goals to attain; you already are love, light, beautiful, miraculous, worthy, and more. You don't have to feel defeated anymore because you already won. Let your tears flow; you don't have to fight to make them stop because you already won. You are bountiful and magnificent; you are everything and everything is you. There's nothing you need to say or do because you now know and own that you already won.

You don't need a quote, a boat or a book you wrote to win because you already won. From this place inside of yourself, you know that you are the quote, the boat, the book, the sun, the moon, and the stars. You know and own that you were born a winner and you know and own that everyone was born a winner too. You now see everything as a reflection of you; therefore, you have more of you to love and more of you to give.

You are a WINNER, so celebrate every moment as such.

The Awakened Winners

Own the truth of who and what you are; you are a winner, so breathe it, live it, love it and be it. YOU WON RIGHT HERE AND RIGHT NOW; YOU WON. YOU ALREADY WON.

I want you to read this so many times. I want you to feel the joy that comes with remembering the truth. I am a winner and so are you. We didn't come here to prove ourselves; we came to be ourselves. To be the unique individual that we are. Celebrating every breath with a smile because we are alive.

That we don't miss out on our lives, chasing it but that we embrace our existence. Human beings, believing in themselves. Walking on the Earth with respect, love and devotion because we remember we are love and loved. We now dance freely knowing we won before we were born.

There's no match for the feeling that comes with knowing that we've already won. Celebrate it, dance it, sing it, breathe it, live it and love it…

YOU ALREADY WON!

Acknowledgments

Thank you God and the Goddess within, for the privilege of existence. I'm grateful to know myself as love and as one with you. The Temple gates of my heart are open, and because of you, I get to love the way that you love me, and I am emotionally grateful for that. Thank you for the privilege of seeing life through your eyes. Life is so Beautiful! Thank you. Thank you. Thank you. I Love You So Much.

I also want to thank myself for showing up the way that I do. Like many of you, I have felt defeated, and I have chosen to look at myself deeply, and I am so glad that I have and continue to. I am so grateful to be exactly who I am. I remember a time when I was afraid to say this but I'm not afraid anymore, I Love Myself Beyond Measure.

Nicholis Cordon (my son). My life would not be the same without you in it. I was lost before you came into the world. You gave me a reason to love more than I could have ever imagined. You are such a gift to me, and I'm grateful every second of the day that God blessed me with your presence. I Love you So Much, and I'm devoted to being the best that I can be for you always—your momma!

Lola Bella (my dogter). I didn't know I could love a dog as much as I love you. Your presence has helped expand my capacity to love. I truly couldn't have asked for a better loyal companion. You are my baby girl, and I love you so much!

Mother (Rosa Rosario). I am truly blessed to have the privilege of calling you Mom. Thank you for being such a devoted and loving mother. I know raising seven girls wasn't easy, but you did it. I want you to know that you have inspired me simply by loving us the way that you did and do. I Love You So Much and I appreciate you more than you know.

Father (Luis Dominguez). I am so proud to be your daughter. Your presence in my life is invaluable, and I am grateful for everything you have done and continue to do for our family. Thank you for being so passionate about loving our family and for giving us the best of you. I love you so much, and I am beyond grateful for you!

Thank you, Rose Stokes, for being exactly who you are. You have an incredibly beautiful heart. I'm grateful that my dad met you and that you were open and willing to take my family in as your own. And now it is your own, you are our family, and I'm so grateful for that. Thank you for everything you've done and continue to do. I love and appreciate you so much!

Thank you to my six sisters, Nitza Holland, Carmen Dominguez, Marta Dominguez, Mildred Dominguez, Emily Dominguez, and Vanessa Dominguez, for being part of the light in my heart. My heart would not be shining as bright as it does without your part of the spark. I am so grateful that God gifted me the opportunity to share my life with all of you. Through the good, the bad, and the ugly, we have persevered, and I am beyond grateful for that. I Love You So Much!

Thank you to my nieces and nephews for being exactly who you are. To say that I am a proud aunt is an understatement. I am so proud to call all of you, my family. You remind me that I am blessed beyond measure, simply because you exist. I Love You All So Much: Melissa Anaya, Shalimar Quiles, Jordan Fonseca, Yashana Rivera, Kyana Rivera, Marlon Rivera, Arianna Devoe, Kyra Devoe, Michael Caban Jr., Isaiah Caban, Nyasia Caban, Maliah Caban, Elyssa Acosta, Jenayah Acosta, Alexis Arias, Ava Arias, Ahmar Romero, Kayden Nunez and to those that have yet to be born, this is for you too, I Love You So Much!

Thank you to my Best Friend, Casandra Rocker. You have been so much more than a friend to me; you are my family. Thank you so much for always supporting my visions and for being my right hand when I needed one. I am so unbelievably grateful for your presence in my life. I Love You So Much!

Thank you Kym Silva for being such a great friend. I appreciate and love you so much.

Acknowledgments

Lastly, I want to thank everyone who has crossed my path. Some of you are still on it, some of you will be, and some of you have come and gone. And no matter what the case may be, I want you to know that I am grateful for your presence in my life because it made a difference. Thank you for being exactly who you are.

About the Author

Loida Dominguez is the CEO of a Women's Empowerment brand called InPower Love Coaching. In her business she helps women better identify themselves with the present moment, so that they can feel empowered by their decisions and live a life of freedom created by choice. She is a single mom of a 16-year-old boy by the name of Nicholis. Her son was born with Down Syndrome, and he is the light of her life. She is a devoted and loving mother that creates change in the way people perceive individuals that need extra support. She offers a perspective of unconditional love and is committed to this being her life's journey.

Loida is transformational in all things. She is an author, a transformational speaker and coach, she is a singer/songwriter, an artist, a sister, a friend, a loving mother and she's a woman devoted to being the change she wants to see in the world.

She has studied the human mind, soul and spirit for years searching for answers. What was revealed to her was more than she could have ever asked for. She loves that she now gets to share her message with the world, so that many more people awaken to the winner that they are.

For more information, check out Loida's website www.theawakenedwinners.com, where you will find details on one-on-one coaching, workshops, retreats and more. You can also find The Awakened Winners page on Facebook and Instagram .

Thank You For Trusting Me With Your Heart.

Namaste

Loida Love Dominguez

THE AWAKENED WINNERS

We already Won